BRIDGE TECHNIQUE SERIES

DECEPTIVE

CARD PLAY

David Bird • Marc Smith

MASTER POINT PRESS • TORONTO

Copyright © 2000 David Bird & Marc Smith

Master Point Press
331 Douglas Ave
Toronto, Ontario, Canada
M5M 1H2
(416) 781-0351   Internet www.masterpointpress.com

Distributed in the USA by Barricade Books
150 Fifth Avenue, Suite 700
New York, NY 10011
(800) 59-BOOKS

Canadian Cataloguing in Publication Data
Bird, David, 1946-
Safety plays

(Bridge technique; 5)
ISBN 1-894154-25-8

1. Contract bridge - card play. I. Smith, Marc, 1960- . II Title. III. Series: Bird, David, 1946-. Bridge technique; 5

GV1282.3 B573 2000   795. 41'.53   C00-931457-1

Cover design and Interior: Olena S. Sullivan
Editor: Ray Lee

Printed and bound in Canada

1 2 3 4 5 6 7   07 06 05 04 03 02 01 00

CONTENTS

Bridge Technique Series

Available Now

Entry Management

Tricks with Trumps

Safety Plays

Eliminations and Throw-Ins

Deceptive Card Play

Planning in Suit Contracts

Available March, 2001

Planning in Notrump Contracts

Defensive Signaling

Squeezes for Everyone

Available September, 2001

Planning in Defense

Reading the Cards

Tricks with Finesses

Choosing the Correct Honor Card

If the defenders knew which cards you held, they would defeat many more contracts than they do. Keeping the defenders in the dark, thereby making their life as difficult as possible, is an important part of the game. In particular, there is nearly always a right and a wrong card to play from honors of equal rank. That's the subject of this chapter.

Selecting from touching honors

When deciding which of touching honors to play, you should aim to create ambiguity in the mind of at least one defender. Suppose you are playing in a spade contract and this is one of the side suits:

♡ 7 6

♡ J 9 8 4 3   ♡ Q 10 2

♡ A K 5

West leads the ♡4 and East plays the queen. Should you win with the king or the ace? Since they are equals, you might wonder how it could possibly matter. It does!

Winning with the ace leaves both defenders in doubt about the position of the king. If, instead, you win with the king, both defenders can be certain that you also hold the ace. West will know because his partner failed to play the ace to the first trick. East will know because his partner would not have underled an ace against a suit contract. Conceding such gratuitous information at Trick 1 may enable a defender to place his partner with a key card in another suit, and therefore find the killing switch when he regains the lead.

Let's suppose now that you hold the king and queen instead.

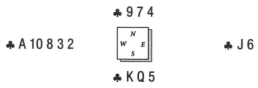

♣ 9 7 4

♣ A 10 8 3 2   ♣ J 6

♣ K Q 5

West leads the ♣3 against your notrump contract, East playing the jack. If East is likely to gain the lead later, it may be right to allow the jack to win (breaking the link between the defenders). Assuming you are going to win the trick, though, should you do so with the king or the queen?

To work out the answer, put yourself in West's position. If the jack loses to the queen, what will he know about the position of the king? Right, he will know that you have it. If East held something like ♣KJ6, he would have played the king instead of the jack. By contrast, if you take the first trick with the king, the location of the queen remains a mystery. West may be tempted to continue the suit when he gains the lead.

The situation is similar when you hold the queen-jack:

♠ A 7 4

♠ K 9 8 3 2   ♠ 10 6

♠ Q J 5

West leads the ♠3. You play low from dummy and East follows with the ten. If you win with the jack, West will know that you also hold the queen. Unless he suspects that your remaining honor is bare, and can be pinned, he will not continue spades when he gets in. By capturing the ten with the queen instead, you leave West in the dark with regard to who holds the jack. He may elect to play his partner for this card, and hand you a third spade trick.

It is truly amazing how many declarers give away a strong holding in a suit by playing a lower honor card than they should. This is a typical situation:

$\diamond$ 5 4

$\diamond$ 8 6 3

$\diamond$ K 9 7 2

$\diamond$ A Q J 10

East switches to the $\diamond$2 and declarer thoughtlessly plays the ten, winning the trick. Now East knows there is no future in the suit. West has a pretty good idea, too! If declarer plays a more sensible queen, the defenders may persevere with the suit later. It's the same if declarer plays the suit himself, leading a low card from dummy. He should finesse the queen, not the jack or the ten.

The general rule has become clear, then:

To disguise your holding, play the top of touching honors.

Sometimes two cards of equal value are on view, in the dummy:

♠ A Q 5

♠ J 9 8 4 2

♠ 10 6

♠ K 7 3

West leads the four of spades. Playing either the ace or the queen leaves some doubt in East's mind about the location of the king. If instead you win the trick in hand with the king, the lie of the suit is exposed.

When you are weak in some other suit and fearful of a later switch in that direction, you may make the same play from this holding:

♠ A Q 5

♠ K 9 8 4 2

♠ 10 6

♠ J 7 3

If you run the ♠4 to your jack you will score three spade tricks, it's true. You will also tell the defenders that there is little future for them in the suit, encouraging them to switch to your weak suit. Play dummy's queen instead and the defenders may not be willing to give up their chances in spades. If it is West who gains the lead first, he may even revive your third trick in the suit!

The same logic applies even when you may not win the trick with the card played:

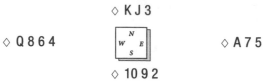

♢ K J 3

♢ Q 8 6 4   ♢ A 7 5

♢ 10 9 2

West leads the ♢4, either in a suit or notrump contract. Which card should you play from dummy?

Your play will hardly matter if East holds the queen. When he has the ace, though, you may wish to encourage a diamond return rather than an awkward switch elsewhere. The best move is to play dummy's jack. When East wins with the ace he may persevere with the suit, placing his partner with the Q-10.

Exceptions to 'high from equals'

It's a harsh fact of bridge life that most rules have exceptions. We have already looked at this situation, where hearts were a side suit in a spade contract:

♡ 7 6

♡ J 9 8 4 3   ♡ Q 10 2

♡ A K 5

You win East's queen with the ace, to disguise the position of the king. Now suppose that you are playing in notrump. Ask yourself how you would normally play if you held ♡A52 rather than ♡AK5. Would you not hold up your ace until the third round? In notrump, it's strange but true that by winning Trick 1 with the ace, you tell both defenders that you also hold the king. Winning with the king instead conceals the position from East. Might his partner not have led from a suit heading by the ace-jack?

Until now we have been attempting to disguise a strong holding. When your intention is the opposite, to appear stronger than you actually are, it may suit you to give away information deliberately by playing the lower of touching honors. Look at this position:

◇ 9 7 4

◇ A 10 8 3 2   ◇ J 6 5

◇ K Q

West leads the three to his partner's jack. You would like to persuade West that you hold a double stopper, to deter him from laying down the ace when he gains the lead. The best chance of doing this is to win with the queen, deliberately letting West know that you also hold the king. When West comes on lead he may try to reach his partner's hand for a lead through your king. Of course, an astute defender may ask himself why you have given away such gratuitous information! Where bluffs are possible, so are double bluffs. Against an expert West you might choose to win with the king anyway.

The situation is the same here:

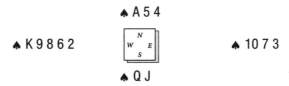

♠ A 5 4

♠ K 9 8 6 2   ♠ 10 7 3

♠ Q J

West leads the ♠6 against a notrump contract. If you win East's ten with the queen, West may be encouraged to lead the spade king when he gains the lead. Win instead with the jack, letting West know that you hold the queen, and he may be reluctant to make such a play.

Sometimes you must tailor your deceptive play to the perceived standard of the opponents. Look at this position:

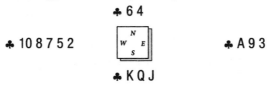

♣ 6 4

♣ 10 8 7 5 2   ♣ A 9 3

♣ K Q J

You are playing in notrump and wish to appear weak in this suit because you are poorly protected in some other suit. When West leads the ♣5 to East's ace, it is tempting to drop the queen on the first round and to win the second round with the king. When you subsequently lose the lead to East, he may conclude that his partner has led from a jack-high holding and the remaining clubs are ready to run.

That's fine against an East who does not watch the spot cards too closely. Put a strong player in the East seat and he will apply the Rule of Eleven to West's ♣5 lead. This will tell him that declarer holds three cards higher than the five. The third card can only be the jack and East may well ask himself why you are bothering to falsecard. Against such a competent opponent you would do better to play the jack on the first round, then win the next round with the queen. East may then conclude that his partner led from king-fifth and is holding up the king to maintain communications.

Encouraging or discouraging a cover

Suppose you have this uninteresting-looking trump suit:

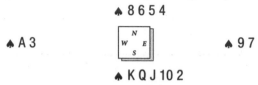

You may think it can scarcely matter which of your trump equals you play on the first round. On some deals, though, you may want West to duck the first round of trumps. (Maybe you have a hidden long side suit and are afraid of a ruff, or perhaps you hope to endplay West with the ace of trumps.) If you lead the king, West will surely slap his ace on the table. Lead the queen instead and you plant a seed of doubt in his mind. We have all hopped up with the ace in this situation, only to see partner's bare king come crashing down!

When playing combinations of this sort, remember the following tips:

Play the lower of equals when you want a defender to duck.
Play the higher of equals when you want him to cover.

Always remember that good deceptive play must be subtle. You want to paint a false picture of your hand in the defenders' mind. The best way to do so is not with a six-inch decorator's brush. An artist does not paint the sea orange because that is not believable. He can, however, convince you with any shade of green or blue. So, to lead the ten from K-Q-J-10 would be taking a good thing too far. West will know that you have higher cards than that, and may well suspect that you are trying to slip the trick past him.

This same idea can work in reverse too. Let's put a similar trump suit into the context of a full deal:

Both Vul.
Dealer West

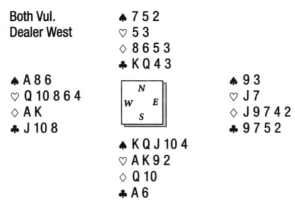

```
                ♠ 7 5 2
                ♡ 5 3
                ◇ 8 6 5 3
                ♣ K Q 4 3
♠ A 8 6                          ♠ 9 3
♡ Q 10 8 6 4      N              ♡ J 7
◇ A K         W       E          ◇ J 9 7 4 2
♣ J 10 8          S              ♣ 9 7 5 2
                ♠ K Q J 10 4
                ♡ A K 9 2
                ◇ Q 10
                ♣ A 6
```

West opens 1♡ and you bid all the way to 4♠. How should you play the hand when West cashes two diamonds and switches to the ♣J?

You can throw one heart loser on dummy's clubs but the other will have to be ruffed. To maximize your chance of avoiding an overruff from East, you would like to draw precisely two rounds of trumps before attempting a heart ruff. Your best chance of achieving this goal is to persuade West to take his ace on the first round of trumps. So, win the club in hand and lead the king of trumps at Trick 4. If West mistakenly takes this trick, you can safely negotiate a heart ruff. Lead any other trump honor except the king and there is a greater chance that West will hold up the ace. He will then be in a position to draw two more rounds if you continue the suit.

Sometimes a cover by a defender will cause a blockage in one of declarer's suits. Suppose you need five tricks from this club suit and you have no outside entry to dummy:

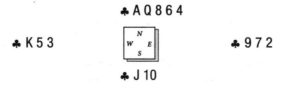

```
            ♣ A Q 8 6 4
                   N
♣ K 5 3        W       E        ♣ 9 7 2
                   S
            ♣ J 10
```

Your only chance is to find the suit breaking 3-3 with West clutching the king. Even then, West can stymie your plans by playing his king on the first round of the suit. How can you reduce the chance of West finding this defense?

If you lead the jack first, West will surely cover. This would be the winning defense if his partner held ♣10xx. A better bet is to lead the ten. West may now duck, hoping that you will run the card to East's presumed jack and allow him to make a damaging play.

Similarly, suppose you need four diamond tricks from this combination with no outside entry to dummy:

◇ A K Q 3

◇ J 7 6 4  ◇ 8 5 2

◇ 10 9

You need West to hold the jack but it will not suit you if he plays it on the first round — the suit will be blocked. If you lead the ten West will often cover, particularly if his jack is doubleton or tripleton. Advance the nine instead and you will catch many a West asleep at the helm.

So, leading the higher of touching honors is more likely to elicit a cover. If you do not want a cover, play the lower card.

Sometimes you want to encourage a cover by the defender in the third seat:

♡ Q 10 5

♡ 8 7 6 3 2  ♡ K 9 4

♡ A J

West leads the ♡3 against a notrump contract. If East holds the king, you would like him to play it — giving you three heart tricks. The best chance of persuading him to do this is to play dummy's queen at Trick 1.

This position is similar:

♡ Q 5

♡ 7 4 2  ♡ K 8 6 3

♡ A J 10 9

West leads the ♡4 against a spade contract. Again you should put up the queen, tempting East to cover. Play low from dummy and he is more likely to hold up the king.

Making intermediate cards pull their weight

It often happens that the opening lead gives you a two-way guess. There may be a tactical advantage in guessing one way rather than another. Ask yourself: how much will the defenders know about the suit if my guess fails? Here is a familiar position:

♣ J 6 4

♣ ? 8 5 2   ♣ ? 7 3

♣ A K 9

West leads a fourth-highest ♣2 against a notrump contract. Would you try dummy's jack or run the lead to your nine?

Say that you play low and East produces the ten. You win with the ace, but West now knows that you started with A-K-9. He will not continue the suit, should he gain the lead.

Suppose, instead, that you hop up with the jack and East covers with the queen. West will not know who holds the nine. When he gets in, he may continue spades, hoping that his partner holds that card.

You can put a nine to a different use in this position:

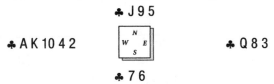

♣ J 9 5

♣ 10 7 6 4 2   ♣ Q 8 3

♣ A K

When West leads the ♣4 you should insert dummy's nine; if East covers you will score three club tricks. It is easy to criticize East for covering but from his seat, in notrump, the suit might lie like this:

♣ J 9 5

♣ A K 10 4 2   ♣ Q 8 3

♣ 7 6

Partner would unimpressed if East allowed dummy's nine to win! In a suit contract East may be worried that the suit lies like this:

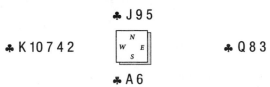

♣ J 9 5

♣ K 10 7 4 2   ♣ Q 8 3

♣ A 6

If he fails to cover the nine, declarer will lose no trick in the suit. While it is true that declarer can always make two club tricks after the lead, he may have no useful discard or the defense may be able to establish sufficient tricks to set the contract by then.

Playing the nine from J-9-x in dummy may be productive in this layout too:

```
                    ♠ J 9 5
                   ┌─────┐
  ♠ 10 7 6 4 2     │ N   │    ♠ K 8 3
                   │W   E│
                   │  S  │
                   └─────┘
                    ♠ A Q
```

If you play the five instead there is more chance that East will reach for his eight.

There are many similar positions:

```
                    ♠ J 10 5
                   ┌─────┐
  ♠ K 8 7 4 2      │ N   │    ♠ Q 9 6 3
                   │W   E│
                   │  S  │
                   └─────┘
                    ♠ A
```

If East covers dummy's jack, the ten is promoted into a stopper.

Key points

1. When winning with touching honors in the closed hand, it is usually right to win with the top card. For example, holding K-Q-7, you win East's jack with the king. From West's point of view, East may then hold the queen.

2. When your touching honors are bare, it may be advantageous to let the defenders know that you hold two honors. For example, with a stopper of K-Q doubleton in notrump, you might choose to win East's jack with the queen.

3. Before leading touching honors from the closed hand, ask yourself if you want your left-hand opponent to cover. If the answer is 'Yes', lead your top honor. If 'No', the second-highest card is better.

4. Similarly, play a high card from dummy when you want to encourage the defender in the third seat to expend an honor.

5. Remember that the picture you are trying to create in a defender's mind must be consistent with what he already knows about the hand.

QUIZ

A.   ♣ 7 6

♣4 led

```
       N
   W       E
       S
```

♣10 played

♣ A Q J 2

Playing in notrump, do you win with the queen or the jack? Why is one card better than the other?

B.   ♡ 10 6 4

♡2 led

```
       N
   W       E
       S
```

♡ A K 9

How will you play this suit (in notrump) if you are weak in a different suit and wish to deter a switch?

C.   ♠ A J 5

♠4 led

```
       N
   W       E
       S
```

♠ K 10 6

Which card should you play from dummy? (Assume that the use of the spade suit for entry purposes is not relevant.)

D.   ◇ 10 9 6

◇7 led

```
       N
   W       E
       S
```

◇ A J 4

Playing in a spade contract, East gains the lead and switches to a high diamond intermediate. Which card should you play from your hand?

E. ♠ J 7 5 2

♠ A K 9 6 4 3

How do you play this trump suit for no loser?

F. ♡ A 7 6 3

♡ J 10 9 8 5 2

How do you try to play this suit for no loser?

G. ◇ A K 4 3

◇ J 10

With no outside entry to dummy, what is your best chance of scoring three diamond tricks?

Answers

A. If you capture East's ten with the jack, West will know that your holding is headed by the A-Q-J and that a continuation will cost a trick. Win with the queen instead and he may be tempted to continue the suit, hoping that his partner holds the jack.

B. The important case is when the two missing honors are split. Let's say this is the position:

♡ 10 6 4

♡ Q 8 5 2   ♡ J 7 3

♡ A K 9

If you play low from dummy, East will force the ace or king by putting in the jack. West will then know that you started with A-K-9. When he subsequently regains the lead, he will not lead away from his queen for a second time.

By rising with dummy's ten, you create the possibility in West's mind that his partner holds J-9. Indeed, such a scenario may seem probable and he is likely to continue hearts when he gets in.

C. When West has led from the queen, it will make little difference what you do. When East holds that card, however, you can cause some confusion. You should play the jack from dummy. If this is covered by the queen and king, neither defender will know who holds the ten. When they gain the lead, they may persevere with spades, rather than switching to more promising territory. Indeed, if you take the second round with the ace, your deception will not be uncovered until the third round.

D. West can tell from his partner's card that you hold both the ace and jack. By playing the jack on the first round, you may persuade him that you hold ◊ AJ doubleton. He may then be tempted to return the suit. If instead you play your low card, he will know that he must switch.

E. The only interesting case is where East holds Q-10-8. Lead the jack from dummy on the first round. You have no intention of running the jack but you may tempt a sleepy opponent to cover! If he does, you can then return to dummy in some other suit and finesse the nine.

F. This time you have no chance — right? True, but if you don't at least try, you will never get lucky. This is the layout you are looking for...

♡ A 7 6 3

♡ Q 4   ♡ K

♡ J 10 9 8 5 2

If you lead the jack, you might tempt West into a fatal cover. If he does not rise to the occasion, then you are no worse off than if you had simply cashed the ace.

If the bidding has not disclosed your length in the suit, another possibility exists. West might cover from a doubleton K-4, fearing that you hold Q-J-x-x.

G. You have no legitimate play for three tricks. Even if the finesse works, West can hold you to two diamond tricks by covering your first lead of the suit. To make it tougher for him, remember the tip: lead a lower card if you do not want the next player to cover. West is likely to cover if you start with the jack. Advancing the ten gives you a much better chance of sneaking past West's queen.

CHAPTER 2

Disrupting the Defenders' Signals

In order to defend accurately, the defenders must signal to each other. The three major types of signal are:

1. *Attitude (high to encourage, low to discourage),*
2. *Count (high to show an even number of cards, low for odd),*
3. *Suit preference (high for the higher remaining suit, low for the lower suit).*

As declarer, there is no need to signal to dummy (except perhaps to tell him what you want from the bar). You are therefore at liberty to select the order in which you play your cards — particularly your spot cards — solely to disrupt the defenders' signals.

You may be surprised to hear that, as declarer, you can use your spot-cards to signal to the defenders! A simple rule is to signal as if you were defending. If you like the lead, play an encouraging high card. If you wish to discourage a continuation, play your lowest card. In the next few sections we will see how and why this works.

Disrupting attitude signals in notrump

Suppose you are playing in 3NT and West leads the king of hearts, asking for an attitude signal:

♡ 10 7 4

♡ A K J 6 3   N W E S   ♡ 9 5

♡ Q 8 2

    East will play a discouraging five. If you follow with the two, it will be clear to West that the five was partner's lowest heart. He will switch to another suit, waiting for East to play a heart through your queen. Try playing the ♡8 on the first trick. West is now in the dark. He cannot tell whether East's five is an encouraging card from Q-5-2 or a discouraging card from 9-5. He may elect to continue hearts, setting up your queen and breaking the link between the defenders.

    This is the other side of the coin:

♡ 10 7

♡ A K J 6 3   N W E S   ♡ Q 5 4

♡ 9 8 2

    West leads the king and East encourages with the five. If you misguidedly falsecard with the nine or eight, it will be clear to West that his partner has played an encouraging signal. Your only hope is to play the two, leaving open the possibility (in West's eyes) that East has played a discouraging five from 9-5 or 8-5.

    What can we conclude from this? When you wish to encourage or discourage a continuation, as declarer, you should signal in just the same way as the right-hand defender would. You should play a high card to encourage a continuation, a low card to discourage.

    One word of warning. When signaling with a high card, do not choose too high a card. Look at this position:

♡ 10 7

♡ A K J 8 3   N W E S   ♡ 9 4

♡ Q 6 5 2

    West leads the ace and East discourages with the four. Your correct card, to encourage a continuation as declarer, is the five. This leaves open the possibility that East has encouraged from Q-4-2. Suppose instead that you play the six. Any bright West will ask: where is the five? East cannot hold it or he would chosen that card to make his supposed encouraging signal as clear as possible. West will therefore know that you hold the five and are attempting a deception.

To encourage, you should choose the card that is higher than the defender's signal but closest to it.

Disrupting attitude signals in a suit contract

The same technique can be applied when declaring a suit contract, particularly when a ruff is threatened. Say you are playing in 4♠ with this diamond suit:

♢ Q 9 6 3

♢ A K J 4   N W E S   ♢ 7 2

♢ 10 8 5

West leads the ace, asking his partner for an attitude signal. When East follows with the seven, you can see that a ruff is imminent. You do not want a diamond continuation, so play your lowest card — the five. West will note that the two is missing but his partner's seven may be a discouraging card from 10 8 7 (declarer falsecarding the five).

As before, if you misguidedly try to confuse the issue by following with the eight or the ten, you kill the only ambiguity from West's point of view. He will have no problem cashing the king and delivering the ruff.

Now let's switch the South and East holdings:

♢ Q 9 6 3

♢ A K J 4   N W E S   ♢ 10 8 5

♢ 7 2

West attacks with the ace of diamonds, and East follows with the five. This time, you want West to cash the ace, setting up dummy's queen for an early discard. By playing the seven at Trick 1, you may persuade West that his partner has begun a high-low signal from ♢ 5 2.

Note that this piece of trickery is more likely to succeed with certain card combinations. The most effective position is the one shown, when the two-card holding has the lowest and the third-lowest spot-card. If East held ◇1075 and you played the eight from ◇82, West would be less inclined to read partner for 5-2 doubleton. 'Why should declarer play the eight if he held 10-8-7?' he might ask himself. That should not stop you from trying, though!

An 'encouraging signal' from declarer can improve the prospects of a Bath Coup:

◇ 6 3

◇ K Q 10 8 4   ◇ 9 5

◇ A J 7 2

West leads the ◇K and the standard Bath Coup involves a hold-up in the hope that West will continue the suit into your tenace. Give West a small push by following with the seven from your hand. He may then read partner for A-5-2 or J-5-2.

Using honors to encourage a continuation

It is not only small cards that can be used to create a false impression of your holding. Suppose you are playing in notrump and West attacks your stronghold here:

♣ K Q

♣ 10 8 7 4 2   ♣ 9 6 3

♣ A J 5

West leads the four of clubs and East follows with the three, playing attitude signals. Nothing you do will persuade West that his partner has the ace of clubs. However, by playing the jack under dummy's honor at Trick 1 you create the impression that you hold ♣AJ doubleton. The defenders may then persist with the suit, rather than switching to a weak point elsewhere.

This particular deception would not work against defenders who play count signals on their own leads. East's ♣3 would proclaim three clubs, exposing South's jack as a falsecard.

This is a similar position:

♠ Q 10 4

♠ K 9 7 6 2

♠ 8 3 2

♠ A J 5

West leads the ♠6 against your 3NT. You rise with the queen in an attempt to smoke out the king, but East plays a discouraging three. Following with the jack from your hand may cause West to place you with A-J bare. He may subsequently continue spades, expecting your ace to come down. You will then score a third spade trick.

Once again, this will not work against defenders who use count signals. East will play the eight on the first round, telling West that you have a third spade. Such count signals are useful even when no deception is involved. Suppose dummy holds Q-J-10 and one of these cards wins the first trick. East's count signal will let his partner know if declarer's ace is now bare.

Here is a further variation:

◇ J 10 4

◇ Q 9 7 6

◇ 8 3 2

◇ A K 5

West leads the ◇6 and you cover with dummy's jack. If East plays the queen you plan to win with the ace, hiding the king. When East in fact plays low, you can overtake with the king, feigning ace-king bare.

Holding up to discourage a continuation

No deception is involved in the common position in the next diagram.

♡ J 10 4

♡ 7 6

♡ K Q 9 5 3

♡ A 8 2

East has opened 1♡ and you are now playing in notrump. West leads the ♡7. You play the ten from dummy and allow East to win the trick with the queen. East cannot continue the suit now. Even if a key finesse into the West hand loses, your contract will be safe.

A key to successful deception is to make the same play on different holdings. Bear the above situation in mind as you tackle 3NT:

Neither Vul.
Dealer East

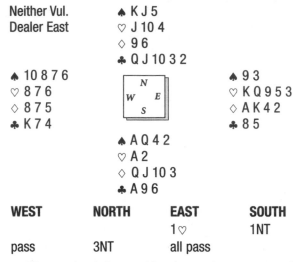

♠ K J 5
♡ J 10 4
◇ 9 6
♣ Q J 10 3 2

♠ 10 8 7 6
♡ 8 7 6
◇ 8 7 5
♣ K 7 4

♠ 9 3
♡ K Q 9 5 3
◇ A K 4 2
♣ 8 5

♠ A Q 4 2
♡ A 2
◇ Q J 10 3
♣ A 9 6

WEST	NORTH	EAST	SOUTH
		1♡	1NT
pass	3NT	all pass	

West will open the defense with a heart, the exact spot depending on the East-West lead agreements. You cover with dummy's ten and East plays the queen. What now?

If the clubs come in for five tricks it will not matter what you do. What if West has the ♣K, though? In that case, taking your ♡A at Trick 1 will prove fatal. So, duck smoothly and leave East to puzzle out how the heart suit lies. On the actual hand, he can defeat the contract by returning a low heart to your now-bare ace. When West gets in with the ♣K, he will play his third heart and you will go three down.

East is likely to place you with ♡Axx after your 1NT overcall, however, particularly after the duck at Trick 1. In that case he may cast his net elsewhere, switching to a low diamond.

A similar situation would also apply if dummy had ♡Q10x. With ♡Axx in hand, it would be sound technique to play an honor from dummy, allowing East to win the trick. By playing the same way when your ♡A is doubleton, you may encourage East to switch at Trick 2.

Disrupting count signals

The defenders rely on count signals when they need to hold up a stopper to kill a long suit in dummy. As declarer, you can often steal an extra trick by interfering with those signals. Say you have this club suit:

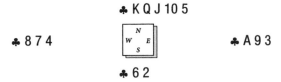

♣ K Q J 10 5

♣ 8 7 4   ♣ A 9 3

♣ 6 2

You are playing in a notrump contract and dummy has no outside entry. If you start by leading the ♣2, then West (playing standard count signals) will follow with the four. East will know that his partner started with an odd number of clubs (three or one) leaving you with two or four. Since East's play makes no difference when you hold four clubs, he will take his ace on the second round, restricting you to the minimum number of club tricks when you hold a doubleton.

Observe how much more difficult it is for East if you start by leading the ♣6. Again, West will follow with the four and the king will be allowed to win. When you continue with the queen from dummy, East will be unable to tell whether you hold two or three clubs. His partner would play the four from both ♣42 and from his actual holding of ♣874. East may well decide to play safe, withholding his ace on the second round. A second club trick may be enough to give you the contract.

Note that it is essential to lead the second round of clubs from dummy. East then has to make the key decision before seeing a second card from you or West.

Suppose now that East holds four clubs to the ace:

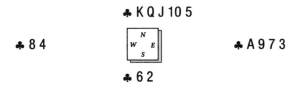

♣ K Q J 10 5

♣ 8 4   ♣ A 9 7 3

♣ 6 2

It still does not cost you to lead the six. The play does not disguise West's ♣8 signal to any useful effect, but East will still have a guess to make when you lead the second round from the dummy. You might have led the six from 6-4-2.

Let's look at the case where you hold three cards in your hand and would like the defense to take the ace on the second round:

◇ K Q J 10

◇ A 6 4   ◇ 9 5 3

◇ 8 7 2

Again, there is no outside entry to dummy. If the first round of diamonds goes: 2-4-K-3, the defenders will have no problem, whichever of them holds the ace. So, you must lead the seven on the first round.

Your next play depends on who you think holds the ace. If you think West has it, you should return to your hand in a different suit and lead the eight. If West thinks that his partner played the three on the first round from 9-5-3-2, he may take his ace prematurely. (Many defenders agree to echo with the second-best card, here the five, to avoid such a situation.) If instead you think that East holds the ace, you must lead the second round of diamonds from dummy. In both cases your aim is the same — to force the defender with the ace to make his decision before seeing further spot-cards from the closed hands.

Disrupting suit preference signals

When defenders deliver a ruff, they will usually indicate the preferred suit of return by the size of the card they lead. A high spot card will suggest the lead of the higher remaining side suit, a low spot card the lower suit. Sometimes you will have the opportunity to create doubt in the defender's mind. Look at this deal:

Neither Vul.   ♠ K 10 3 2
Dealer North   ♡ K Q 10 9 8 6
           ◇ K 6
           ♣ 8

♠ J 8 5   ♠ 6
♡ 2   ♡ A J 4
◇ J 10 7 4 2   ◇ Q 9 8 3
♣ J 9 7 4   ♣ A 10 5 3 2

           ♠ A Q 9 7 4
           ♡ 7 5 3
           ◇ A 5
           ♣ K Q 6

WEST	NORTH	EAST	SOUTH
	1♡	pass	1♠
pass	2♠	pass	4♠
all pass			

West leads the ♡2, covered by the king and ace. A lead of dummy's main suit is always suspicious and you can be fairly sure that West has a singleton heart and is seeking a ruff. No falsecard is available to disguise West's holding, so you should direct your attention towards deflecting a second ruff, which will defeat the contract. This will be possible only if East holds the ♣A and suggests such a return with a suit preference signal.

See what happens if you follow to the first trick with the three. East will win the ♡A and return the ♡4 for his partner to ruff. Knowing that this is East's lowest spot-card, West will play a club back. A second ruff will follow, defeating the contract.

Your only chance is to hide the ♡3, hoping to disguise the fact that East is returning his lowest card for the ruff. So, follow with the ♡5 on the first round and play the ♡7 on the second. Now West cannot read his partner's ♡4 with any certainty. Perhaps it is from ♡A43 and East is playing his top spot-card, requesting a diamond return.

Hiding a spot card

Sometimes, concealing a spot-card will prevent a defender from giving you a nasty guess. Suppose you are playing in a suit contract with this club position:

<pre>
                    ♣ 9 8 2
                   ┌──────────┐
                   │   N   │
    ♣ J 7 6 4   │ W   E │   ♣ A K 5
                   │   S   │
                   └──────────┘
                    ♣ Q 10 3
</pre>

It is a routine deceptive position for East. His partner leads the four of clubs (playing fourth-best leads). A competent East will take the trick with the ace and, if you follow suit with the three, will smartly return the five through your tenace. Since he would defend in exactly this manner if he held ♣AJ5, you will have an unpleasant guess to make. Guess wrongly and the defense will have stolen a trick.

See the difference if you follow with a deceptive ten on the first round of clubs. Now East dare not underlead his remaining honor. This would cost a trick if you held the expected Q-10 doubleton.

Hiding a spot-card can be beneficial in another situation. Look at this hand:

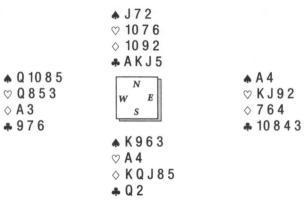

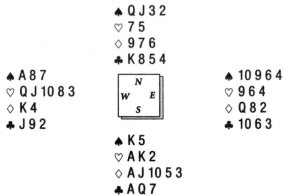

West leads the ♠5 against your 3NT contract, East winning with the ace. If you follow with the three, East will know that his partner holds only four spades and may find the killing switch to hearts. Play the ♠6 instead and East will place his partner with five spades, encouraging him to persevere with the suit.

Using the defenders' count signals

Occasionally, you will be able to use the defenders' count signals for your own benefit. If you feel up to the challenge, take the South seat and cover the defenders' cards on this next deal:

West leads the ♡Q against 3NT and you win with the king. How will you play the contract?

If clubs are 3-3 and you have four club tricks, you can bring your total to nine simply by knocking out the ♠A. In the more likely case that clubs are 4-2 or worse, you would have to play for four diamond tricks (since there is only one entry to dummy, you would need to find East with both diamond honors or one honor doubleton).

So, perhaps you should test the clubs first? The trouble with playing three rounds of clubs is that you will remove the sole entry to dummy. If clubs are 3-3, a hold-up of the defenders' ♠A will deprive you of the two spade tricks you need.

Let's try something else — leading the ♣Q at Trick 2! The defenders don't know that you hold the ace and are therefore both likely to give a true length signal. When the two and the three hit the table, it is a good bet that clubs are 3-3. You should then lead the ♠K, followed by another spade if the ace is held up. If instead some higher club pips appear, you can assume that the clubs are 4-2. You will cross to the ♣K and try your luck in the diamond suit.

Deflecting a ruff

As declarer, it will often be obvious that you are about to suffer a ruff. It may not be quite so clear to the key defender, though. Your general aim will be to disguise your own length in the suit, thereby making it look as if the leader holds more than one card.

This is the play at its simplest:

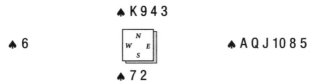

East has made a jump overcall in spades and West's ♠6 lead against your heart contract is therefore likely to be a singleton. East wins with the ten and you drop the seven. Your intention is to make West's holding appear to be 6-2 doubleton. On this particular layout the play is quite likely to succeed. East will not want to have his ♠A ruffed, thereby setting up dummy's king. If instead you play a lazy ♠2, East will be in no doubt that the lead is a singleton.

Sometimes, you may need to sacrifice an honor in the interests of avoiding a ruff. Say East opens with a preemptive 3♡ and you subsequently become declarer in 6♠. West leads the ♡5 and, to your horror, this is the layout:

♡ J 8 4 3

♡ 5   ♡ A Q 10 9 7 6

♡ K 2

After East's preempt, you can be certain that West's lead is a singleton. Your only chance is to drop the K♡ at Trick 1. If East takes your king as a true card (playing his partner for ♡52 doubleton), he may be fearful of continuing the suit, since he might be setting up dummy's jack for a discard.

When you hold three cards in the suit led, you must consider your play carefully. You must choose a card that leaves your left-hand opponent with a plausible holding.

♡ K 7 5 3

♡ 10   ♡ A Q 8 6 2

♡ J 9 4

Hearts are a side suit in a trump contract, and West leads the ten to his partner's queen. Which card should you play from the South hand to prevent the impending ruff?

You should play the jack, leaving open the possibility that West began with ♡1094 and that your jack is singleton. If instead you follow with the nine or the four, East will know that you hold at least two hearts, and he will probably cash the ace next. West will show out and East will deliver the killing ruff.

Try the next position yourself. Which card would you play from hand to deflect a possible ruff?

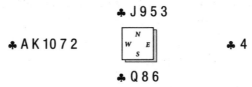

♣ J 9 5 3

♣ A K 10 7 2   ♣ 4

♣ Q 8 6

West leads the ♣A against your spade contract. It makes no difference to you whether East's four is a singleton or from 4-2 doubleton. Either way, the defenders have a ruff to take. Furthermore, the position will be clear to West as soon as he cashes his king. You must therefore find a way to prevent him from doing so.

Your only chance is to play the queen under the ace at Trick 1. If the suit is distributed as shown, then West may take your queen at face value and switch, playing his partner for ♣864.

Even if East actually began with ♣42, West may be persuaded to switch. He will know that something is afoot, since the two is missing. Might not the layout be something like:

$$♣ J 9 5 3$$

$$♣ A K 10 7 \qquad \boxed{\begin{array}{c} N \\ W \quad E \\ S \end{array}} \qquad ♣ 8 6 4$$

$$♣ Q 2$$

Here when West leads the ace, you may be able to encourage a continuation by playing the queen. Thinking that his partner's four was the start of a high-low with a doubleton, West may continue with the king. Only when dummy's jack is set up for a discard, will he switch his line of attack. By then, it may be too late.

If you consistently play the same card from numerous different holdings (in this case ♣Q singleton, ♣Q2 doubleton and ♣Q86) you will make life much tougher for the defense. They will not always do the right thing.

Sometimes the card played from dummy will aid the deception:

$$♣ K J 7 3$$

$$♣ 2 \qquad \boxed{\begin{array}{c} N \\ W \quad E \\ S \end{array}} \qquad ♣ A 10 9 6 4$$

$$♣ Q 8 5$$

You hope to convince East that his partner has led from the queen, so put in the jack from dummy. Contribute the eight from hand and East will place his partner with Q-5-2. A continuation into dummy's tenace will not look very attractive.

Disrupting upside-down signals

Until now, we have assumed that the defenders were playing standard attitude and count signals. It tournament play, at any rate, you will encounter defenders would play their signals the other way round (low to encourage or to show an even number of cards, high to show the opposite). As declarer against such opponents, you must follow the same method!

Let's consider one of the basic situations again, this time with the defenders playing upside-down attitude signals.

♡ 10 7 4

♡ A K J 6 3  ♡ 8 5

♡ Q 9 2

West leads the ace against a notrump contract and East plays a discouraging eight. If you 'cleverly' falsecard with the nine, it will be obvious to West that his partner has a lower heart and is therefore discouraging a continuation. Instead you should play an encouraging (upside-down) card — the two. Now West may misread the position. Perhaps his partner was encouraging from ♡Q98, leaving you with ♡52 doubleton. West may continue the suit to your advantage.

As a general principle, declarer should use the same signaling methods as his opponents — high to encourage when they are playing standard signals, low to encourage when they are using reverse signals.

Key points

1. As declarer, you should play high-low to encourage a continuation and low to discourage — just as you would when defending. If the opponents are using upside-down signals, then you must follow the same method.

2. Playing an unnecessary honor from your hand on the first round of a suit may persuade the defenders that you are short there. (For example, with K-x in dummy and A-Q-J in hand, you might win with dummy's king and drop the queen from hand.) The defenders may persevere with this suit later, missing a profitable switch.

3. Hiding a spot-card may stop the defenders from getting a count by the time they have to make the critical decision. They may give you an extra trick by failing to take their stopper on the optimal round.

4. You may be able to use the defenders' count signals to your advantage. Put yourself in the defenders' seat, and imagine how you would react in certain situations.

5. When a ruff is imminent, you can sometimes cause the defender to misread the situation. By hiding a low spot-card, for example, you may make a singleton lead look like a doubleton.

A.
♣ Q J 10 8 3

```
  N
W   E
  S
```

♣ 7 2

In a notrump contract, with no outside entry to dummy, what is your best chance of scoring a club trick?

B.

♥10 led

♥ A K

```
  N
W   E
  S
```

♥ Q J 4

Declaring a notrump contract, which card should you play from hand if you want the defense to continue this suit when they regain the lead?

C.

♠3 led

♠ K 7 4 2

```
  N
W   E
  S
```

♠ J 10 9

West leads the three of spades against your heart contract. You play low from dummy, and West wins with the queen. Which card should you play from your hand?

D.

♦2 led

♦ Q 6 3

```
  N
W   E
  S
```

♦ K J 8 4

Playing in a spade contract, East opens with the two of diamonds and East takes the ace. Which card should you play from your hand?

Answers

A. Your best chance is that the suit is distributed something like this:

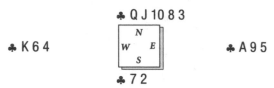

♣ Q J 10 8 3

♣ K 6 4

♣ A 9 5

♣ 7 2

Lead the seven from hand. West cannot afford to take his king in case you hold ♣Axx (or ♣xxx, in which case East would not subsequently be able to hold up his ace until the third round). He will therefore signal his length with the four. Because you have concealed the two, East cannot tell whether his partner started a high-low from ♣42, or has played low from his actual holding.

If instead you lead the two, it will be easy for East to take the ace. The only holdings from which his partner would play the four would be ♣K74, ♣K64, ♣764 or singleton ♣4.

B. You should follow with the jack. If the defenders are playing count signals, you cannot fool West, as he will be able to tell from his partner's card that you hold three hearts. However, East will have no clue to the count. If you have a choice of which defender to allow in first, it should therefore be East. When the opponents are playing attitude signals, this falsecard may deceive either defender. East would play a discouraging card with three or four low hearts.

C. You should play the ten, leaving open in East's eyes the possibility that the opening lead was from J-9-3. West would have led the top of his sequence from either ♠J103 or ♠1093, so no other play from the South hand will present East with a problem.

D. Your best chance is to follow with the king. East may then play his partner for ◇J842 and you for the singleton king. This cannot cost a trick, since one of your winners would otherwise be ruffed at Trick 2 anyway.

CHAPTER • 3

Feigning Strength or Weakness

The most important deceptive plays are those designed to disguise your holding in the suit the defenders have led.

You may wish to conceal your strength there, to encourage a continuation. You may instead wish to create an impression of strength, hoping that the defenders will switch their attention elsewhere. In Chapter 1 we discussed how you could take advantage of touching honors to good effect in this respect. In this chapter we consider other methods of deception. We will also look at some particular situations in which you may need to cloak your holding.

Feigning weakness to hide the location of losers

The more information the defenders have, the more likely they are to defend accurately. It follows that you should put them to the test as early as possible during the play. Suppose the opening lead is made in a suit that you plan to establish, in order to dispose of some losers. It may pay you to feign weakness in the suit by ducking the opening lead.

This is the type of deal we have in mind:

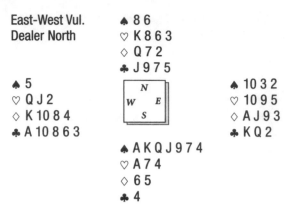

East-West Vul.
Dealer North

North:
♠ 8 6
♡ K 8 6 3
♢ Q 7 2
♣ J 9 7 5

West:
♠ 5
♡ Q J 2
♢ K 10 8 4
♣ A 10 8 6 3

East:
♠ 10 3 2
♡ 10 9 5
♢ A J 9 3
♣ K Q 2

South:
♠ A K Q J 9 7 4
♡ A 7 4
♢ 6 5
♣ 4

Rightly or wrongly, you open 4♠ in the third seat. There is no further bidding and West leads the ♡Q. Suppose you win with the ace, draw trumps in two rounds, then duck a heart. Competent defenders, playing count signals, will surely collect their three tricks in the minors and you will be one down.

Try something different — ducking the first trick! Add to the effect by playing the seven from your hand, making East's five look like an encouraging signal. When West's ♡Q wins the first trick, he will probably play another heart. You can then win with the ace, draw trumps, and take a discard on dummy's long heart. The key to success was to put West to his critical decision early in the play, before he had much information on the hand.

See if you can spot a similar play on this deal:

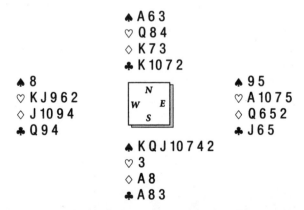

North:
♠ A 6 3
♡ Q 8 4
♢ K 7 3
♣ K 10 7 2

West:
♠ 8
♡ K J 9 6 2
♢ J 10 9 4
♣ Q 9 4

East:
♠ 9 5
♡ A 10 7 5
♢ Q 6 5 2
♣ J 6 5

South:
♠ K Q J 10 7 4 2
♡ 3
♢ A 8
♣ A 8 3

West leads the jack of diamonds against 6♠. If you win the opening lead, draw trumps, and set up a club winner, the most moderate defenders in the world will cash their heart trick. Once again your best chance is to duck the opening lead. If West fails to find the heart switch, the slam is yours. After drawing trumps, you will throw a club on the third round of diamonds and ruff the long club good for a heart discard.

Feigning weakness to avoid a switch

When you are playing in notrump with one suit completely bare, desperate measures may be needed to avoid a switch to the unguarded suit.

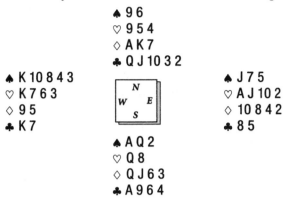

```
                    ♠ 9 6
                    ♡ 9 5 4
                    ◇ A K 7
                    ♣ Q J 10 3 2
  ♠ K 10 8 4 3                        ♠ J 7 5
  ♡ K 7 6 3          N                ♡ A J 10 2
  ◇ 9 5         W         E           ◇ 10 8 4 2
  ♣ K 7              S                ♣ 8 5
                    ♠ A Q 2
                    ♡ Q 8
                    ◇ Q J 6 3
                    ♣ A 9 6 4
```

Partner raises your strong notrump to game and West leads the ♠4 to East's jack. Let's suppose first that you win with the queen, cross to the ◇A, and run the ♣Q. When West wins with the king, he may conclude that you will have nine tricks on a spade continuation. A switch to hearts will then beat the contract.

Suppose instead that you capture East's ♠J with an unnecessarily high card — the ace. If West places his partner with the queen of spades he may continue with a low spade on winning the club king. You will then be good for ten tricks.

West may be suspicious that you did not hold up in spades but that is not conclusive evidence of a falsecard from A-Q-x. Perhaps you held A-x-x in spades and only A-x in hearts. In that case you would win the spade lead immediately for fear of a heart switch. In any case there would be little benefit in a spade hold-up when the key club finesse was into the West hand.

On the actual hand, a heart switch by West could put the contract four down. It would also produce a silly result if East did hold ♠QJx and declarer had the ♡A. So, is there a way for West to cater for both possibilities?

Yes, but it requires considerable partnership trust and understanding. At Trick 4, West should lay down the ♠K. If East does indeed hold the queen, he should unblock it under the king, allowing West to cash three more winners in the suit. If instead East follows with a low spade, West should assume that declarer holds the queen and switch his attack to hearts. Only in this way will he beat the contract in both cases.

Let's see another example of feigning weakness in the suit led:

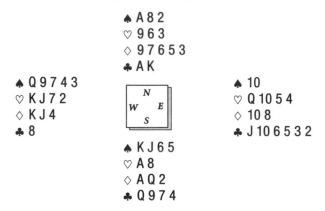

```
                    ♠ A 8 2
                    ♡ 9 6 3
                    ◇ 9 7 6 5 3
                    ♣ A K
    ♠ Q 9 7 4 3                      ♠ 10
    ♡ K J 7 2          N             ♡ Q 10 5 4
    ◇ K J 4        W       E         ◇ 10 8
    ♣ 8                S             ♣ J 10 6 5 3 2
                    ♠ K J 6 5
                    ♡ A 8
                    ◇ A Q 2
                    ♣ Q 9 7 4
```

West leads the ♠4 against 3NT. Suppose you simply win East's ten with the jack, cross to a club honor, and finesse the queen of diamonds. West will see little future in a spade continuation and will doubtless switch to hearts, beating the contract.

A better idea is to win the spade lead with dummy's ace, continuing with a diamond finesse. If West concludes that you would not rise with the ace holding king-jack in your hand, he may persevere with spades.

The scheme that works best as the cards lie is to play low from dummy and to win East's ten with the king. West will then place his partner with the ♠J. When you cross to a club honor and finesse the diamond queen, he will surely continue spades. You will then have time to set up the diamond suit.

If the ten and nine of spades were interchanged, however, it would not be convincing to win the nine with the king. West would know, from his partner's failure to play the card, that you held the ♠J too. Nor would any deception be possible if you played low from dummy and East produced the queen. All in all, the best deceptive move in the long run is to rise with the spade ace.

Feigning strength to resolve a guess

When declarer leads towards a king in the closed hand, there are at least two reasons why the defender to his left may choose not to win with the ace. Perhaps the suit lies like this:

$$\heartsuit\ 7\ 5\ 2$$

$\heartsuit\ A\ 9\ 4$

	N	
W		E
	S	

$\heartsuit\ J\ 8\ 6\ 3$

$$\heartsuit\ K\ Q\ 10$$

If West takes the king with the ace, declarer will finesse the ten on the next round and score two tricks in the suit. If instead West allows the king to win, declarer may return to dummy and try his luck with a heart to the queen.

Or, perhaps declarer is in a slam with this club holding:

$$\clubsuit\ 7\ 5\ 2$$

$\clubsuit\ A\ 9\ 4$

	N	
W		E
	S	

$\clubsuit\ J\ 10\ 8\ 3$

$$\clubsuit\ K\ Q\ 6$$

If the king loses to the ace, declarer may take a successful finesse in a different suit for his twelfth trick. If the king is allowed to win, he will have to guess which suit to play on. Since many defenders would have taken the ace if the card sat over the king, he is likely to play on clubs again. Another possible reason to refuse to capture a king in the closed hand is that by winning the trick you may rectify the count for declarer, allowing him to perform a squeeze.

You may wonder how we can justify such a lengthy preamble on holding up aces that sit over kings. The reason is that when you are playing against defenders who are capable of such a hold-up, you can turn their defensive skill to your advantage. Look at this deal:

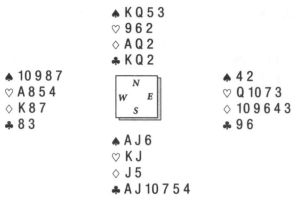

```
                ♠ K Q 5 3
                ♡ 9 6 2
                ◇ A Q 2
                ♣ K Q 2
 ♠ 10 9 8 7          N          ♠ 4 2
 ♡ A 8 5 4      W        E      ♡ Q 10 7 3
 ◇ K 8 7            S           ◇ 10 9 6 4 3
 ♣ 8 3                          ♣ 9 6
                ♠ A J 6
                ♡ K J
                ◇ J 5
                ♣ A J 10 7 5 4
```

You arrive in 6NT and West leads the ♠10. You have eleven top tricks and it seems you must guess which of three red-suit finesses to take. Should you play for the ◇K, the ♡A, or the ♡Q to be onside?

The correct answer is not even close. For sure, each chance individually is 50%. If you only intend to take one of the finesses, then it matters little which one you choose. Wouldn't it be nice to be able to combine some of your chances?

By far the best chance of success is to win the opening spade lead in dummy and immediately play a heart to the king. If the ace is onside or West holds up the ace for one of the reasons outlined above, you will have your twelfth trick. Even if West wins with the ♡A, you will still be able to take a diamond finesse unless West continues with a second heart.

Suppose you were playing the same cards in a contract of 6♣. Another deceptive line would be possible. Win the spade lead with the ace and advance the ◇J! Caught unawares, very few Wests would be capable of playing low smoothly when they held the king. If West does play low, with no reaction, you will win with dummy's ace, draw trumps, and throw the remaining diamond on the fourth round of spades. You can then take a guess in the heart suit, combining the chances in diamonds and hearts.

Feigning strength to encourage a switch

Playing in notrump, you will sometimes have the opportunity to play on a suit where you are completely bare. If the defenders believe that you are trying to establish some tricks in this suit, they may be deterred from cashing their winners there. Even better, they may switch to a different suit, giving you an extra trick. Look at this deal:

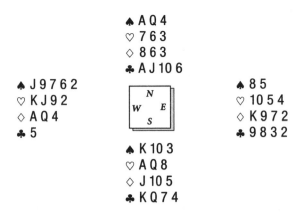

```
                    ♠ A Q 4
                    ♡ 7 6 3
                    ◇ 8 6 3
                    ♣ A J 10 6
♠ J 9 7 6 2                          ♠ 8 5
♡ K J 9 2          N                 ♡ 10 5 4
◇ A Q 4        W       E             ◇ K 9 7 2
♣ 5                S                 ♣ 9 8 3 2
                    ♠ K 10 3
                    ♡ A Q 8
                    ◇ J 10 5
                    ♣ K Q 7 4
```

After bidding of 1NT - 3NT, West leads the ♠6. There are eight top tricks and the ♡Q represents your only serious chance of a ninth. A direct heart finesse will give you a 50% chance and most players would be content with that. Let's try something different, however. Win the spade lead with the ten and cross to dummy with the ♣J, letting West know that you are well at home in that suit. Then play a diamond to the jack!

If West places you with something like K-J-10-x in diamonds, he is likely to switch to a heart at top speed. He knows that there is no future for the defenders in the black suits and may assume that his only hope is find East with the ace or queen of hearts. 'Just the nine,' you will say, as you casually face your cards.

Feigning length or shortness

In the previous chapter we saw how you can deflect a ruff by feigning shortness in the closed hand. Sometimes it will suit you to feign length. instead. Take declarer's seat here and look at the heart situation:

Neither Vul. ♠ K J 6 3
Dealer East ♡ K Q 7 2
             ◇ A Q 5
             ♣ Q 7

♠ 7 4   ♠ —
♡ J 8 3   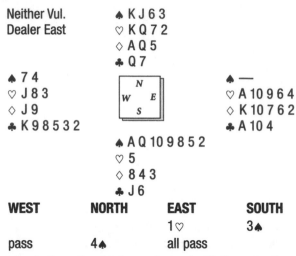   ♡ A 10 9 6 4
◇ J 9   ◇ K 10 7 6 2
♣ K 9 8 5 3 2   ♣ A 10 4

             ♠ A Q 10 9 8 5 2
             ♡ 5
             ◇ 8 4 3
             ♣ J 6

WEST	NORTH	EAST	SOUTH
		1♡	3♠
pass	4♠	all pass	

West leads the ♡3, which you know is likely to be from length.
From East's point of view, however, the lead might well be a singleton.
Bearing this in mind, how would you play the contract?

Most players would contribute a heart honor from dummy, without
thinking about it. Whether East returned another heart or played ace
and another club, the contract would hinge on the diamond finesse —
destined to fail. However, you know that West has led from either J-x-x
or 10-x-x. If it is the former, you can give East a real headache by playing a low heart from dummy at Trick 1! The objective is to persuade
East that you hold the ♡J (and therefore the missing length in the suit).
If East falls for this, he will surely win with the ♡A and attempt to give
his partner a heart ruff — to be followed by ♣A and a second ruff. He
will be swiftly disillusioned when you throw a club on his heart return.
You can now score an overtrick, in fact, by discarding both clubs, elim-
inating clubs, and eventually throwing East in with a fourth round of
hearts (a loser-on-loser play, throwing a diamond).

Suppose instead that you held J-8-5 of hearts and therefore knew
that West's ♡3 lead was a singleton. You would feign shortness in the
suit by rising with the king and playing the eight from hand. If East read
his partner for J-5-3 in the heart suit, he might switch his attention elsewhere.

When you need to take a discard on a side suit with five cards in the
dummy, three in your own hand, it will not suit you if a defender ruffs
the third round and cashes a winner or two. Sometimes deception can
come to your rescue. Look at this deal:

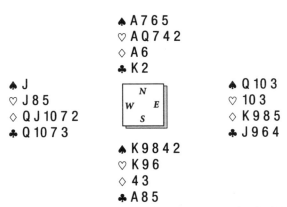

```
            ♠ A 7 6 5
            ♡ A Q 7 4 2
            ◇ A 6
            ♣ K 2
♠ J                        ♠ Q 10 3
♡ J 8 5                    ♡ 10 3
◇ Q J 10 7 2               ◇ K 9 8 5
♣ Q 10 7 3                 ♣ J 9 6 4
            ♠ K 9 8 4 2
            ♡ K 9 6
            ◇ 4 3
            ♣ A 8 5
```

You reach 6♠ and West makes the troublesome lead of the diamond queen. You take the ace and cash two top trumps, revealing that East has a trick in that suit. You now need to discard your diamond loser on dummy's heart suit before East can trump in. When East has only two hearts, as in the diagram, he will be able to ruff the third round and cash a diamond. Can you see how to deflect him from this winning defense?

You must persuade East that you also hold only two hearts. Win the second round of spades in hand with the king and 'finesse' the queen of hearts. (No, we do not recommend that you mutter 'That's lucky' when the queen wins!) Next, cash the ♡A and play a third round. If East thinks that his partner started with ♡KJxx he may discard on the third round of hearts, rather than allow you to throw a loser as he ruffs with his master trump. Your king scores and you re-enter dummy with the ♣K. When you then lead the fourth round of hearts, East is powerless — you will throw your diamond loser whether he ruffs or not.

Finally, feigning shortness can persuade the defenders to miscount the tricks available to them. Declarer on the following deal, from a match between England and Northern Ireland, was maestro Terence Reese:

North-South Vul.   ♠ K 9 8 6
Dealer West   ♡ Q 3
                ◇ A 9 3
                ♣ A Q J 3

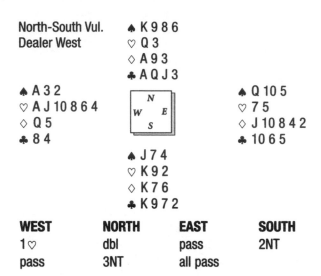

♠ A 3 2   ♠ Q 10 5
♡ A J 10 8 6 4   ♡ 7 5
◇ Q 5   ◇ J 10 8 4 2
♣ 8 4   ♣ 10 6 5

                ♠ J 7 4
                ♡ K 9 2
                ◇ K 7 6
                ♣ K 9 7 2

WEST	NORTH	EAST	SOUTH
1♡	dbl	pass	2NT
pass	3NT	all pass	

How would you play 3NT after West leads the ♡J?

Reese won with the dummy's queen and dropped the ♡9 from his hand, feigning shortness.   When he later played a spade towards dummy, West hopped up with the ace and, placing South with an initial ♡K9, attempted to cash his heart suit. Declarer's ♡K became the ninth trick.

Critics at the time blamed West for failing to observe his partner's ♡5 attitude signal. He would not have played this from ♡752, they claimed, so declarer's nine was bound to be a false card. Nowadays it is more common for the defenders to play count signals. East would show an even number of hearts by playing the seven and declarer's deception would be unmasked. Fear not, you will still find defenders by the thousand who fall for such ploys!

Key points

1. When the defenders fail to find the best opening lead against a notrump contract, avoid making this failure obvious. If you feign weakness in your attacked stronghold, they are less likely to find the killing switch at their next opportunity.

2. Force the defenders to make the key decision early in the hand, before they have the chance to signal.

3. Avoid revealing your true holding in a suit. Try to play different suit combinations in a manner that looks the same to the defenders. Unable to tell which of two or three possible holdings you have, they will frequently do the wrong thing.

4. By looking at the problem from the defender's angle, you may visualize how you can present him with a guess.

A.

♠ 6 3
♡ 7 6
◇ A K 7 5
♣ J 9 6 5 3

```
      N
  W       E
      S
```

♠ A 5
♡ A K J 3
◇ Q 8 3
♣ Q 10 8 7

WEST	NORTH	EAST	SOUTH
			1♣
1♡	3♣	pass	3NT
all pass			

West leads the ♡5, East playing the ten. How do you plan to give yourself the best chance of making nine tricks?

B.

♠ A 9 3
♡ Q 10 7 2
◇ J 10 6 3
♣ A 4

```
      N
  W       E
      S
```

♠ 6 4
♡ K J 4
◇ A 8 2
♣ K Q 8 5 2

WEST	NORTH	EAST	SOUTH
			1NT¹
pass	3NT	all pass	

1.   12-14.

West leads the ♣3. Plan the play. If you play low from dummy, East will play the ten.

Answers

A. If you capture East's ten of hearts with the jack, it will be clear to West that the defense has no future in that suit. If he wins the first club trick, he is sure to table a spade. You want West to continue hearts, so encourage him to do so by winning Trick 1 with the king. When he comes on lead, West will assume that his partner holds the ♡J. He will continue with the ♡Q, in case his partner started with ♡J10 doubleton. With your tenuous spade stopper intact, you will have time to establish the clubs. (If East wins the first club and returns a heart, you will win with the ace. Your remaining J-x will still protect the heart suit from attack by West.)

B. Once West has led a club, prospects of a 3-3 break in the suit are poor. It looks as though West holds something like ♣J973 and East ♣106. You could capture the ten with your queen and later concede a trick to West's jack, but the chances are that the defenders will, by then, have worked out where their strength lies. A better strategy is to allow East's ♣10 to win at Trick 1. In itself though, that is not enough. You want East to continue clubs, so make him think that his partner has the five-card suit. Follow with the ♣5 under his ten. Unless he can see that a switch is obvious, the chances are that East will return a second club, giving you the time to set up the heart suit.

Creating a Losing Option

Declarer can cause the defenders many a problem simply by leading towards the closed hand. Let's look at the first example from the defender's seat. Suppose you are East here, defending a spade contract:

♡ Q 7 5 3

 ♡ A 10 6 2

The ♡3 is led from dummy. You decide to play low and declarer wins with the king, partner playing the four. Dummy is re-entered in a different suit and another low heart is played. What do you do?

The answer is that you cannot tell with any degree of certainty. If declarer started with K-J doubleton and you hold up the ace again, you may let through an impossible contract. If you rise with the ace and partner has the jack, however, you will set up dummy's queen.

On the next combination you are playing in 3NT and need four club tricks. Can you see how to give the defense a similar problem?

♣ A Q 8 5 2

♣ 7 4 3

Most declarers would take a first-round finesse of the queen, not imagining that any other play was possible. They fail to appreciate the problems that East may face if the first play is a low club from the table. Suppose he has ♣K6 or ♣K10. Fearing that you hold the jack, he may save you a trick by going in with the king. Nor will he be any better off if he thinks for a while, considering whether to play the king. You would then drop his king on the next round. East's situation is all the more difficult because he will not have been expecting you to play a low club from dummy.

If East places you with the jack, he may regard the suit as a lost cause even when he holds something like K-10-x. He may rise with the king, taking the opportunity to clear the defenders' main suit.

Creating an imaginary loser

Persuading a defender that he can defeat the contract by grabbing a winner can produce bushels of points. Suppose the defenders lead a club against a suit contract and this is your holding:

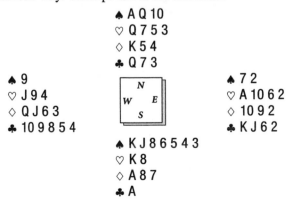

You would play the queen from dummy, hoping that West had led from the king.

Suppose instead that you hold a singleton ace in the South hand. Can you see any advantage in playing dummy's queen now? You may convince the defenders that you have a loser in the suit. This can gain in more than one way. Perhaps this is the full hand:

```
              ♠ A Q 10
              ♡ Q 7 5 3
              ◇ K 5 4
              ♣ Q 7 3
♠ 9                          ♠ 7 2
♡ J 9 4         N            ♡ A 10 6 2
◇ Q J 6 3    W     E         ◇ 10 9 2
♣ 10 9 8 5 4    S            ♣ K J 6 2
              ♠ K J 8 6 5 4 3
              ♡ K 8
              ◇ A 8 7
              ♣ A
```

You play in 6♠ and West leads the ♣10. There are some legitimate chances. You could try to squeeze a defender who holds five diamonds along with either the ♣K or four hearts. You can play for East to hold the ♡A not more than twice guarded. As you see, none of these chances materializes. However, you can keep all but one of those options alive while greatly increasing the chance of a defender erring. Try playing the queen of clubs from dummy at Trick 1!

East covers with the king and you take the ace. What will happen, do you think, when you play a trump to the queen and lead a low heart? East will surely jump in with the ace, thinking that he can cash the ♣J. The ♡Q will then provide a parking place for your diamond loser.

The same deceptive play may gain in this situation too:

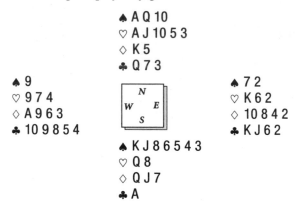

```
              ♠ A Q 10
              ♡ A J 10 5 3
              ◊ K 5
              ♣ Q 7 3
♠ 9                           ♠ 7 2
♡ 9 7 4          N            ♡ K 6 2
◊ A 9 6 3     W     E         ◊ 10 8 4 2
♣ 10 9 8 5 4     S            ♣ K J 6 2
              ♠ K J 8 6 5 4 3
              ♡ Q 8
              ◊ Q J 7
              ♣ A
```

Once more you are in 6♠ and West leads the ♣10 covered by the queen, king and ace. At Trick 2, you run the ♡Q to East's king. The chances are that he will try to cash a club trick rather than find the killing diamond switch.

Note that it would not be a good idea to draw trumps before playing on hearts. West might then have a chance to signal for a diamond switch.

Phantom finesses

If you want to encourage a defender to duck an ace, try to give the impression that you are about to take a finesse against a lesser honor. Suppose you are East here:

♡ J 10 5

   ♡ A 7 6 3

How would you defend when declarer leads the jack from dummy? Usually you will play low, expecting the jack to be run to partner's queen. That would be the correct move if the full deal looked like this:

♠ 7 2
♡ J 10 5
◇ K Q 5
♣ A 8 7 6 2

♠ J 9 6 5 3   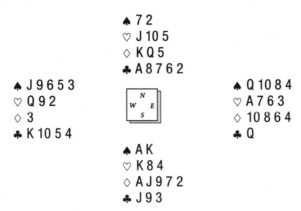   ♠ Q 10 8 4
♡ Q 9 2   ♡ A 7 6 3
◇ 3   ◇ 10 8 6 4
♣ K 10 5 4   ♣ Q

♠ A K
♡ K 8 4
◇ A J 9 7 2
♣ J 9 3

South opens a strong notrump, and North raises to game. West leads the ♠5, and declarer captures the queen with his ace. Declarer can count eight top tricks, so he needs one heart trick to bring his total to nine. Suppose he crosses to dummy with the ◇K and leads the ♡J at Trick 3.

East must play low without giving away possession of the ace. Only if he manages to do this, will declarer have to guess the heart position to make his contract. If East plays the ♡A, or even thinks about doing so, declarer will have no guess to take and the contract will be made.

Playing low smoothly was not such a tough defense for East to find, was it? Ah, but perhaps the actual hand was:

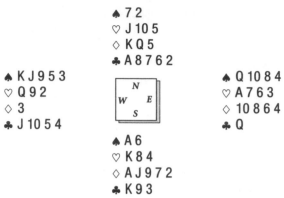

```
              ♠ 7 2
              ♡ J 10 5
              ◇ K Q 5
              ♣ A 8 7 6 2
♠ K J 9 5 3        N        ♠ Q 10 8 4
♡ Q 9 2        W     E      ♡ A 7 6 3
◇ 3               S         ◇ 10 8 6 4
♣ J 10 5 4                  ♣ Q
              ♠ A 6
              ♡ K 8 4
              ◇ A J 9 7 2
              ♣ K 9 3
```

Declarer would play in exactly the same way! This time, though, there is no guess involved. Declarer cannot afford West to hold the ace of hearts because he knows the defenders will cash at least four spade tricks. With the spade suit wide open, his plan is to slip past East's ♡A, scoring a ninth trick with the ♡K before the defenders realize what is happening.

The phantom finesse can be effective here, too:

```
                 ♠ K 9 7
                    N
♠ A 6 5          W     E         ♠ 8 4 3 2
                    S
                 ♠ Q J 10
```

If you need to score just one spade trick without losing the lead, try leading the jack from your hand. West will usually play low instinctively, expecting you to run the jack to his partner's presumed queen. With one spade trick in the bag, you will switch to a different suit, establishing the tricks you need for the contact. Even the best of defenders will go astray if you put them under pressure in this way. Try to put them to the decision before they have much general information about the hand.

Pseudo-finesses

In the previous section, we saw how you could dupe a defender into thinking you were taking a finesse when one did not exist. There is also considerable scope for deception when a finesse position exists but you have no intention of taking it.

Defenders are conditioned to 'cover an honor with an honor'.

That's because it is technically necessary in positions like this:

♠ Q 7 3

♠ 10 8 6   ♠ K 5 4

♠ A J 9 2

If the queen is led from dummy and East does not cover, declarer will score four tricks from the suit. Covering the queen with the king promotes a spade trick for West's ten.

As declarer, you can turn this natural reflex to your advantage. Consider this trump suit:

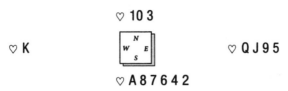

♡ 10 3

♡ K   ♡ Q J 9 5

♡ A 8 7 6 4 2

Essentially, you need a 3-2 heart break in order to limit your losers to two. However, leading the ten from dummy might tempt East into an indiscretion. If he makes the mistake of covering the ten, it will cost him a trick. (An untutored East might cover also from K-Q-9-5 or K-J-9-5.)

Here is another example:

◇ J 6 5 3

◇ —   ◇ Q 10 8

◇ A K 9 7 4 2

It costs nothing to lead the jack from dummy. East should not cover the jack, of course, but that does not mean that he won't. Opponents do not defend perfectly on every hand. They will make even more mistakes if you just give them a chance.

Here is a similar position:

◇ J 6 5 3

◇ K   ◇ Q 10 8

◇ A 9 7 4 2

Aiming for just one loser, the normal play is to cash the ace first (gaining when East has a singleton honor). When this possibility can be discounted — if East opened 1NT, for example — you can try leading the jack from dummy. You will gain by force when West has a singleton ten, and East may cover in the diagramed position also!

There is another, important, gain to be made from leading honors to tempt a cover. You can combine two chances instead of relying on just one. The setting is a grand slam on this example:

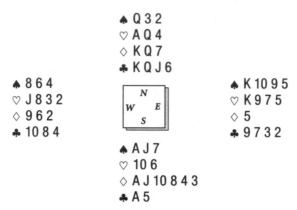

<pre>
              ♠ Q 3 2
              ♡ A Q 4
              ◇ K Q 7
              ♣ K Q J 6
    ♠ 8 6 4   ♠ K 10 9 5
    ♡ J 8 3 2   N   ♡ K 9 7 5
    ◇ 9 6 2   W   E   ◇ 5
    ♣ 10 8 4   S   ♣ 9 7 3 2
              ♠ A J 7
              ♡ 10 6
              ◇ A J 10 8 4 3
              ♣ A 5
</pre>

You play in 7◇ on a trump lead. You can count twelve tricks, but you need a winning major-suit finesse for the thirteenth. Will you finesse in spades or hearts?

Strange as it may seem — in a grand slam — you can combine the two chances against most opponents. Win the trump lead in dummy and play the ♠Q. You have no intention of running the queen, but East cannot tell that. Most defenders, if they hold the king, will either cover instinctively or, at least, make it clear that they thought of doing so.

If the ♠K appears, your problems are over. If East plays low without a flicker the ♠K is almost certainly offside. You will rise with the ♠A and, later, fall back on the heart finesse. Playing in this way, you are likely to succeed if either major-suit king is onside.

Note that it would not be a good idea to draw trumps first. Once East knows that you have a six-card trump suit, he can count you for ten tricks in the minors and the major-suit aces, a total of twelve. He is more likely to diagnose that you have no intention of running the ♠Q.

Slipping past an honor

There is plenty of scope for deception in trump contracts. Suppose this is a side suit in a trump contract:

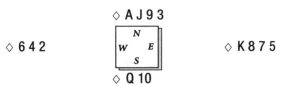

$\diamond$ A J 9 3

$\diamond$ 6 4 2 $\diamond$ K 8 7 5

$\diamond$ Q 10

You lead the queen from your hand and West follows with a low card. West would usually have covered if he had the king, so the odds are high that East holds that card. Try the effect of going up with the ace and leading back the $\diamond$ 3. East may play low now, taking the view that you are trying to ruff the king out in three rounds. Your ten wins the second round of the suit. What's more, you can now score a third diamond trick, without surrendering the lead, by taking a ruffing finesse against East's king.

If the bidding marks East with the king, then you can make it even more difficult for him. Simply cash the ace while in dummy, drop the queen under it, and continue with a low card. Note that the defenders can counter this type of deception by signaling their length to each other. In the situation above, West would play the two on the first round, letting East know that declarer holds a second diamond. It is not always easy for defenders to know when they need to signal, however. If they signal all the time, they will assist declarer in his own reading of the cards.

Take the South cards here and look for a similar deception:

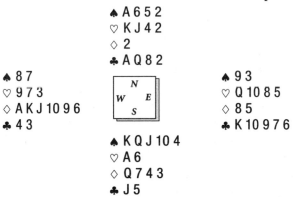

♠ A 6 5 2
♡ K J 4 2
$\diamond$ 2
♣ A Q 8 2

♠ 8 7   ♠ 9 3
♡ 9 7 3   ♡ Q 10 8 5
$\diamond$ A K J 10 9 6 $\diamond$ 8 5
♣ 4 3   ♣ K 10 9 7 6

♠ K Q J 10 4
♡ A 6
$\diamond$ Q 7 4 3
♣ J 5

You play in 6♠ after West has opened with a weak 2$\diamond$ (5-9 points). West leads the $\diamond$ K and switches to a trump. How do you assess your prospects?

If the opponents had not bid at all you would have combined the chances of ruffing out the ♡Q in three rounds with that of a club finesse.

Here the club finesse is known to be wrong and there is little chance either of finding West with the ♡Q or of ruffing that card out trebleton from the East hand.

If East holds the ♡Q and the ♣K you may think he can be squeezed. By the time you have ruffed three diamonds, however, you will have no convenient entry to your hand in order to run the trumps.

The only remaining chance is to resort to subterfuge. Win the trump lead, cross to the ♣A, and play the ♣2! East may scratch his head for a while, but there is a good chance that he will then play low, placing you with a singleton club and perhaps ♡Axx.

The more often you give the defenders a chance to do the wrong thing, the more often they will grab the opportunity with both hands.

Compacting the defenders' trump tricks

Even the best of bidders sometimes arrive in contracts that appear completely hopeless (we speak from experience!). See if you can present the enemy with a losing option on this deal:

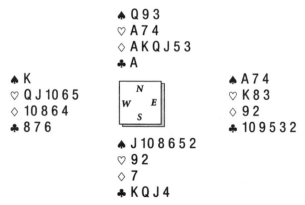

```
              ♠ Q 9 3
              ♡ A 7 4
              ◊ A K Q J 5 3
              ♣ A
♠ K                              ♠ A 7 4
♡ Q J 10 6 5      N              ♡ K 8 3
◊ 10 8 6 4     W     E           ◊ 9 2
♣ 8 7 6           S              ♣ 10 9 5 3 2
              ♠ J 10 8 6 5 2
              ♡ 9 2
              ◊ 7
              ♣ K Q J 4
```

You play in 6♠ after an auction that seemed reasonable at the time. West leads the ♡Q. Can you see any chance?

You start by taking the ♡A and cashing two rounds of diamonds, discarding your heart loser. What next?

Most players would try the effect of leading the queen of trumps, hoping that East would do something silly such as covering from ♠K74.

You need East to err, but there is a much better chance of persuading him to do so. All you need is a little imagination. Let's pretend that your hand is slightly different. Something like:

♠ K J 10 8 6 5   ♡ 9 5 2   ◇ 7   ♣ K Q 4

If that was your hand, what would be your next move?

Right, you would try to cash a third high diamond on which you could dispose of your second heart loser.

On the actual hand, you have no more losers to discard, but East does not know this. You lead a third high diamond and let's say that East ruffs with the four. You overruff, play a club to dummy, and lead the jack of diamonds. In all probability, East will ruff again, with the seven. You are home now. You overruff with the eight and play a trump. The ace and the king come crashing down on the same trick. Be sure to sit well back in your seat, to avoid the sparks that fly between East and West.

Was East's defense so bad? Not really. If you had held the 'Pretend Hand' that we imagined above, East would have needed to ruff twice to defeat the contract.

Key points

1. It is easier for defenders to make the correct play in the key suit if they know how many tricks they need from it. Put them to the test early, before they have the necessary information.

2. When it seems clear that a straightforward finesse is destined to fail, don't take it! With a holding like J-x opposite dummy's A-Q-x-x, play to the ace and return a low card.

3. When you just need to slip a trick past an ace, lead a card that looks like you are about to finesse.

4. Defenders have a natural tendency to cover when an honor is led. Take advantage of this! When an honor is not covered, you can sometimes switch horses and take a different finesse instead.

A.   ♡ A Q 10 6 3

♡ J 2

If this is a side suit in a trump contract and you think East holds the king, how might you bring in the suit without losing a trick?

B.   ♣ K J 7 3

♣ 10 9 6 2

If you can afford to lose a club trick (or two) to West, but you do not want East to gain the lead, how should you set about developing winners in this club suit?

C.   ♠ J 7 3

♠10 led

♠ A K

If you would like the defense to continue this suit when they regain the lead, how should you play?

D.   ◇ A Q 3

◇ J 10 9 4

You think East holds the ◇ K. How will you play the suit to encourage him to win the king on the first round (leaving you with an entry back to your hand)

Answers

A. Play the two to the ace, then lead a low heart from dummy. If East has ♡Kxxx he may decide that you hold a singleton and withhold his king. Your jack will score and you can later take a ruffing finesse against East's king.

B. Start by leading a low club from dummy. If East has the ♣A, you will not be able to keep him out. When he holds ♣Qx, however, he will almost certainly follow low on the first round of the suit. He will expect you to hold the ace and finesse into his queen on the way back. If West wins the first round of clubs with the ace, you will next play to the king, trying to drop the queen from the East hand.

C. Play the jack from dummy at Trick 1, and hope that East can cover with the queen. When you win with the ace you may then persuade West that his partner holds the king. When you win with the king on the second round, the defenders may think that they have a third-round spade trick to cash.

D. Play low to the queen. Since his partner might hold a second trick in the suit, East is unlikely to hold up the king. If instead you run the jack or play ace and another diamond, East will know that you also hold the jack. He may make life awkward by holding up his king.

More Bridge Titles from Master Point Press

Classic Kantar *A collection of bridge humor* by Eddie Kantar
192pp., PB   Can $19.95   US $14.95

Competitive Bidding in the 21st Century by Marshall Miles
254pp.,PB   Can. $22.95   US. $16.95

Countdown to Winning Bridge by Tim Bourke and Marc Smith
92pp., PB   Can $19.95   US $14.95

Easier Done Than Said *Brilliancy at the Bridge Table*
by Prakash K. Paranjape
128pp., PB   Can $15.95   US $12.95

For Love or Money *The Life of a Bridge Journalist*
by Mark Horton and Brian Senior (Foreword by Omar Sharif)
189pp., PB   Can $22.95   US $16.95

I Shot my Bridge Partner by Matthew Granovetter
384pp., PB   Can $19.95   US $14.95

Murder at the Bridge Table by Matthew Granovetter
320pp., PB   Can $19.95   US $14.95

Partnership Bidding *A Workbook* by Mary Paul
96pp., PB   Can $9.95   US $7.95

Playing With The Bridge Legends by Barnet Shenkin
(forewords by Zia and Michael Rosenberg)
192pp., PB   Can $22.95   US $16.95

Saints and Sinners: *The St. Titus Bridge Challenge*
by David Bird & Tim Bourke
192pp., PB   Can $19.95   US $14.95

Tales out of School 'Bridge 101' *and other stories* by David Silver
(foreword by Dorothy Hayden Truscott)
128pp., PB   Can $ 12.95   US $9.95

The Bridge Player's Bedside Book edited by Tony Forrester
256pp., HC   Can $27.95   US $19.95

The Complete Book of BOLS Bridge Tips edited by Sally Brock
176pp., PB (photographs)   Can $24.95   US$17.95

There Must Be A Way... *52 challenging bridge hands*
by Andrew Diosy (foreword by Eddie Kantar)
96pp., PB $9.95 US & Can.

You Have to See This... *52 more challenging bridge problems*
by Andrew Diosy and Linda Lee
96pp., PB   Can $12.95   US $9.95

World Class — *Conversations with the Bridge Masters* by Marc Smith
288pp., PB (photographs)   Can $24.95   US $17.95